SOME POEMS OF FRIEDRICH HÖLDERLIN

BIOGRAPHICAL NOTE

FRIEDRICH HÖLDERLIN was born in 1770 in Württemberg; attended theological seminaries in his youth and studied at Tübingen until the age of 23. For the following nine years he was a tutor in various towns in Germany and Switzerland. In 1801 he journeyed across the mountains of Auvergne to Bordeaux, to become a tutor in a private family there; and half a year later returned by foot to his home in Nürtingen and arrived there destitute, in a state of mild insanity. For the last thirty-six years of his life he lived in Tübingen in the home of Herr Zimmer, a carpenter, in a state of harmless but hopeless madness. He died in 1843, at the age of 73, after a life curiously bleak, empty and solitary.

His greatest poetry was written between the ages of 23 and 30. During his forty years of darkness he wrote occasional verses and fragments which he signed sometimes by the name of Scaliger Rosa, sometimes Scardanelli.

His work is notable for its wonderful rhapsodic clarity, but beneath that lie an extraordinary intelligence and a profound culture, which give to his worship of nature and to his passion for Hellas a quality much more penetrating, more affirmative, and more sonorous than mere nostalgia. His technique avoids any touch of virtuosity or casual impressionism. His vocabulary is simple, broad, generalized. And in his greatest poems he attains a degree of formal control fused with imaginative power and exaltation which is, I think, without parallel in modern times.

The order of the poems which follow is very roughly chronological. The German text, with Hölderlin's own curious spellings, is based on Norbert von Hellingrath's edition, Berlin, 1923. The translations are offered, apologetically, as humble versions of a poetry which uniquely transcends translatability. An effort has been made to adhere with precision to the Greek metres (Alcaic, Asclepiadean) which Hölderlin so religiously observed.

F. P.

Some Poems of
FRIEDRICH HÖLDERLIN

Translated by
FREDERIC PROKOSCH

Friedrich Hölderlin

« The Poets of the Year »

NEW DIRECTIONS : NORFOLK CONNECTICUT

I. AN DIE NATUR

Da ich noch um deinen Schleier spielte,
Noch an dir wie eine Blüthe hieng,
Noch dein Herz in jedem Laute fühlte,
Der mein zärtlichbebend Herz umfieng,
Da ich noch mit Glauben und mit Sehnen
Reich, wie du, vor deinem Bilde stand,
Eine Stelle noch für meine Thränen,
Eine Welt für meine Liebe fand;

Da zur Sonne noch mein Herz sich wandte,
Als vernähme seine Töne sie,
Und die Sterne seine Brüder nannte,
Und den Frühling Gottes Melodie,
Da im Hauche, der den Hain bewegte,
Noch dein Geist, der Geist der Freude sich
In des Herzens stiller Welle regte:
Da umfiengen goldne Tage mich.

Wenn im Thale, wo der Quell mich kühlte,
Wo der jugendlichen Sträuche Grün
Um die stillen Felsenwände spielte
Und der Äther durch die Zweige schien,
Wenn ich da, von Blüthen übergossen,
Still und trunken ihren Othem trank,
Und zu mir, von Licht und Glanz umflossen,
Aus den Höhn die goldne Wolke sank;

Wenn ich fern auf nakter Heide wallte,
Wo aus dämmernder Geklüfte Schooss
Der Titanensang der Ströme schallte
Und die Nacht der Wolken mich umschloss,
Wenn der Sturm mit seinen Wetterwoogen
Mir vorüber durch die Berge fuhr
Und des Himmels Flammen mich umflogen:
Da erschienst du, Seele der Natur!

I. TO NATURE

While your veil lay floating still around me
And I clung to you as flowers cling
And could feel your secret heart surround me
And my trembling heart could hear it sing,
While I still before your image hovered,
Rich, like you, with longing and belief,
And a world for all my love discovered,
And could find a place for all my grief,

While my heart still found a sunward turning,
To the sound of sunlight listening,
And discerned its brothers in the burning
Planets, and the song of God in spring,
While your breath still stirred, and I could hear it
In the swaying forest, and could see
Stirring wavelike in the heart your spirit
And the days of gold encircled me:

Valleys where the spring lay cool and flowing
And the slender saplings in the breeze
Played above the soundless cliffs, and glowing
Daylight glimmered brightly through the trees,
Where I lay among the blossoms, dreaming
Drank their fragrance, overwhelmed and still,
And a cloud of gold, aloft and gleaming,
Slowly from the spires of heaven fell,

When I wandered through the naked meadows
The titanic song of waters cried
From the twilit caverns, and the shadows
Of the night flowed in from every side,
When the tempest with its waves resounded,
Past me through the line of mountains stole,
And I stood among the flames, surrounded,
Nature suddenly revealed her soul!

Oft verlor ich da mit trunknen Thränen
Liebend, wie nach langer Irre sich
In den Ocean die Ströme sehnen,
Schöne Welt! in deiner Fülle mich;
Ach! da stürzt' ich mit den Wesen allen
Freudig aus der Einsamkeit der Zeit,
Wie ein Pilger in des Vaters Hallen,
In die Arme der Unendlichkeit.—

Seid gesegnet, goldne Kinderträume,
Ihr verbargt des Lebens Armut mir,
Ihr erzogt des Herzens gute Keime,
Was ich nie erringe, schenktet ihr!
O Natur! an deiner Schönheit Lichte,
Ohne Müh' und Zwang, entfalteten
Sich der Liebe königliche Früchte,
Wie die Erndten in Arkadien.

Todt ist nun, die mich erzog und stillte,
Todt ist nun die jugendliche Welt,
Diese Brust, die einst ein Himmel füllte,
Todt und dürftig wie ein Stoppelfeld;
Ach! es singt der Frühling meinen Sorgen
Noch, wie einst, ein freundlich tröstend Lied,
Aber hin ist meines Lebens Morgen,
Meines Herzens Frühling ist verblüht.

Ewig muss die liebste Liebe darben,
Was wir lieben, ist ein Schatten nur,
Da der Jugend goldne Träume starben,
Starb für mich die freundliche Natur;
Das erfuhrst du nicht in frohen Tagen,
Dass so ferne dir die Heimat liegt,
Armes Herz, du wirst sie nie erfragen,
Wenn dir nicht ein Traum von ihr genügt.

Often I lay lost in senseless grieving
And the world's own fullness gathered me,
As a river, after endless weaving,
Winds at last into the open sea;
I would hurl myself from the exhausting
Solitude of time and gladly come
To the embrace of the everlasting,
Like a pilgrim to his father's home.

Blessèd be the childish dreams that flourished
Golden in a life of poverty;
What could blossom in the heart you nourished,
What I never won you gave to me.
Nature, in whose long and lamplike radiance
Love could bring her regal fruits to grow
Effortlessly, such as the Arcadians
Brought to harvest centuries ago.

That which moulded me mature and even,
All the world of youth, is dead and gone,
And this heart, which once was filled with heaven,
Now lies sterile as a field of stone;
Ah, the spring now sings to me of sorrow,
Songs which once delighted, comforted,
Vanished is the day and is the morrow,
Spring lies barren in my heart and dead.

Love forever will be doomed to hunger,
What we love is nothing but a shade;
When the golden dreams of youth no longer
Lived, I felt the touch of nature fade.
In your happier days how could you ever
Know how far away your harbor lies?
Home, poor heart, you cannot rediscover
If the dream alone does not suffice.

II. EHMALS UND JEZT

In jüngern Tagen war ich des Morgens froh,
   Des Abends weint' ich; jezt, da ich älter bin,
      Beginn' ich zweifelnd meinen Tag, doch
         Heilig und heiter ist mir sein Ende.

III. AN DIE PARZEN

Nur einen Sommer gönnt, ihr Gewaltigen!
   Und einen Herbst zu reifem Gesange mir,
      Dass williger mein Herz, vom süssen
         Spiele gesättiget, dann mir sterbe!

Die Seele, der im Leben ihr göttlich Recht
   Nicht ward, sie ruht auch drunten im Orkus nicht;
      Doch ist mir einst das Heil'ge, das am
         Herzen mir liegt, das Gedicht, gelungen,

Willkommen dann, o Stille der Schattenwelt!
   Zufrieden bin ich, wenn auch mein Saitenspiel
      Mich nicht hinabgeleitet; Einmal
         Lebt'ich, wie Götter, und mehr bedarfs nicht.

IV. DIE KÜRZE

"Warum bist du so kurz? liebst du, wie vormals, denn
   Nun nicht mehr den Gesang? fandst du, als Jüngling, doch
      In den Tagen der Hoffnung,
         Wenn du sangest, das Ende nie?"

Wie mein Glück, ist mein Lied.—Willst du im Abendrot
   Froh dich baden? Hinweg ists, und die Erd ist kalt,
      Und der Vogel der Nacht schwirrt
         Unbequem vor das Auge dir.

II. ONCE AND NOW

In younger days at dawn I was filled with joy
But wept at sunset; now I am older, now
    Each day begins in doubt yet every
        Ending of day is calming and holy.

III. TO THE PARCAE

Allow one single summer, O mighty ones,
One single fall for the ripening of my song,
    So that more willingly, all filled with
        Sweetness, within me my heart may perish.

Nor can the soul, who fails to fulfill on earth
Her godlike powers, in Orcus below find rest;
    Yet once that holy task which lay so
        Close to my heart, the song, succeeded:

O welcome therefore, hush of the world of shades!
For though the sound of strings can accompany me
    No more, I am content; for once I
        Lived like the gods, and desire now nothing.

IV. BREVITY

"Why then are you so brief? Is it that now you love
Singing less than before? While you were young you found
    In the days of your hope no
        Ending, ever, while still you sang?"

Like my joy is my song. Ah, do you long to bathe
Still at dusk in the glow? Vanished, the earth lies cold
    And the bird of the night now
        Whirs uneasily past your eyes.

V. SOKRATES UND ALKIBIADES

'Warum huldigest du, heiliger Sokrates,
  Diesem Jünglinge stets? kennest du Grössers nicht,
    Warum siehet mit Liebe,
      Wie auf Götter, dein Aug' auf ihn?'

Wer das tiefste gedacht, liebt das Lebendigste
  Hohe Tugend versteht, wer in die Welt geblikt,
    Und es neigen die Weisen
      Oft am Ende zu Schönem sich.

VI. MENSCHENBEIFALL

Ist nicht heilig mein Herz, schöneren Lebens voll,
  Seit ich liebe? Warum achtetet ihr mich mehr,
    Da ich stolzer und wilder,
      Wortereicher und leerer war?

Ach! der Menge gefällt, was auf den Marktplaz taugt,
  Und es ehret der Knecht nur den Gewaltsamen;
    An das Göttliche glauben
      Die allein, die es selber sind.

VII. SONNENUNTERGANG

Wo bist du? trunken dämmert die Seele mir
  Von aller deiner Wonne; denn eben ists
    Dass ich gelauscht, wie, goldner Töne
      Voll, der entzükende Sonnenjüngling

Sein Abendlied auf himmlischer Leier spielt';
  Es tönten rings die Wälder und Hügel nach,
    Doch fern ist er zu frommen Völkern,
      Die ihn noch ehren, hinweggegangen.

V. SOCRATES AND ALCIBIADES

Saintly Socrates, why should you incessantly
    Praise this lad? Do you know nothing superior? Why
      Does your eye gaze upon him,
        Lovingly, as upon the gods?

Who most deeply has thought, loves the most living. He
    Only values the best who has beheld the world,
      And the wise in the end shall
        Often turn to the beautiful.

VI. APPLAUSE

Is not my heart more holy, fairer, more filled with life
    Since I've fallen in love? Why did you honor me
      More when I was more haughty,
        Wilder, wordier, emptier?

Ah, the masses enjoy only the marketplace,
    And the slave can revere none but the masterful:
      Only those who themselves are
        Godlike ever believe in gods.

VII. SUNSET

Where are you? Through the glimmer of twilight still
    Your bliss enthralls my spirit; for only now
      I listened and heard how, rich with golden
        Tones, the enrapturing lad of sunlight

Has played the song of dusk on his heavenly lyre;
    And all around resounded the woods and hills.
      But far away among those pious
        Tribes who still worship him, he has wandered.

VIII. DER MENSCH

Kaum sprossten aus den Wassern, o Erde, dir
Der jungen Berge Gipfel und dufteten
  Lustathmend, immergrüner Haine
    Voll, in des Oceans grauer Wildniss

Die ersten holden Inseln; und freudig sah
Des Sonnengottes Auge die Neulinge
  Die Pflanzen, seiner ew'gen Jugend
    Lächelnde Kinder, aus dir geboren

Da auf der Inseln schönster, wo immerhin
Den Hain in zarter Ruhe die Luft umfloss,
  Lag unter Trauben einst, nach lauer
    Nacht, in der dämmernden Morgenstunde

Geboren, Mutter Erde! dein schönstes Kind;—
Und auf zum Vater Helios sieht bekannt
  Der Knab' und wacht und wählt, die süssen
    Beere versuchend, die heilge Rebe

Zur Amme sich; und bald ist er gross; ihn scheun
Die Thiere, denn ein anderer ist wie sie
  Der Mensch; nicht dir und nicht dem Vater
    Gleicht er, denn kühn ist in ihm und einzig

Des Vaters hohe Seele mit deiner Lust,
  O Erd! und deiner Trauer von je vereint;
  Der Göttermutter, der Natur, der
    Allesumfassenden, möcht' er gleichen!

Ach! darum treibt ihn, Erde! vom Herzen dir
Sein Ubermuth, und deine Geschenke sind
  Umsonst, und deine zarten Bande;
    Sucht er ein Besseres doch, der Wilde!

Von seines Ufers duftender Wiese muss
Ins blüthenlose Wasser hinaus der Mensch,
  Und glänzt auch, wie die Sternennacht, von
    Goldenen Früchten sein Hain, doch gräbt er

VIII. MAN

And scarcely from the waters, O world, had sprung
The summits of the earliest hills, and fresh
And full of evergreen, sweet-smelling,
Deep in the wilderness of the ocean

The first fair islands blossomed; and gladly gazed
The sun-god's eye down over the newly born,
The plants, his never-ending youth's own
Smiling descendants, in you created.

Once lay there, on the loveliest of the isles,
Beneath the vines where tender and calm the air
Surrounds the forest, born in twilit
Dawn which succeeded the balmy darkness,

The fairest of your children, O mother earth:
And now the boy looks up at his parent sun,
And wakes, and tastes, and learns to choose the
Succulent berry, the sacred vine as

His nurse; and soon he is fully grown; the beasts
Avoid him, knowing man for a different kind,
And neither you nor his own father
Does he resemble, for keen and closely

United in him lingers his father's soul
Forever with your earthly delight and grief;
He wishes to resemble nature,
Mother of gods, yes, the all-embracing!

Wherefore, alas, his arrogance then expels
Him from your heart, and all of your offerings
Are futile, and your tender fetters;
Reckless, he searches for something better!

O far from all the blossoming banks of home
And out into the flowerless seas he goes:
And though his groves may glisten brightly,
Laden like stars with the golden harvest.

Sich Höhlen in den Bergen und späht im Schacht
Von seines Vaters heiterem Lichte fern,
    Dem Sonnengott auch ungetreu, der
        Knechte nicht liebt und der Sorgen spottet.

Denn freier athmen Vögel der Walds, wenn schon
Des Menschen Brust sich herrlicher hebt, und der
    Die dunkle Zukunft sieht, er muss auch
        Sehen den Tod und allein ihn fürchten.

Und Waffen wider alle, die athmen, trägt
In ewigbangem Stolze der Mensch; im Zwist
    Verzehrt er sich und seines Friedens
        Blume, die zärtliche, blüht nicht lange.

Ist er von allen Lebensgenossen nicht
Der seeligste? Doch tiefer und reissender
    Ergreift das Schiksaal, allausgleichend,
        Auch die entzündbare Brust dem Starken.

IX. DES MORGENS

Vom Thaue glänzt der Rasen; beweglicher
Eilt schon die wache Quelle; die Birke neigt
    Ihr schwankes Haupt, und im Geblätter
        Rauscht es und schimmert; und um die grauen

Gewölke streifen röthliche Flammen dort,
    Verkündende, sie wallen geräuschlos auf;
        Wie Fluthen am Gestaade woogen
            Höher und höher die Wandelbaren.

Komm nun, o komm, und eile mir nicht zu schnell,
Du goldner Tag, zum Gipfel des Himmels fort!
    Denn offner fliegt, vertrauter dir mein
        Auge, du Freudiger! zu, solang du

He still must dig his caves in the hills, and stare
    Into the pits, remote from the radiant sun,
        Untrue to Helios too, the god who
            Loathes all the servants and mocks at sorrow.

The forest birds can breathe more freely as soon
    As man's own heart expands in its splendor; he
        Who sees the coming darkness also
            Death will discern and will fear him only.

Instilled with a proud, continual fear, he bears
    His arms against all living things; and himself
        Consumes in discord, and the fragile
            Flower of peace is withered early.

Is it not he who still of the living stays
    Most blissful? O, but all the more deeply fate
        Who equalizes all things also
            Tears the inflammable heart of the mighty.

IX. IN THE MORNING

The lawn is bright with dew; and more quickly now
    The wakened stream is running; the birch tree nods
        Her supple head, and all her foliage
            Rustles and shimmers; and yonder, high on

The dusky clouds go rippling the scarlet flames:
    Proclaimers, they ascend and without a sound
        Like tides along the shore they billow
            Higher and higher, forever changing.

O come now, come and do not hurry away
    Too soon, O golden day, to the peaks of heaven!
        More clearly, more serenely, happy
            One, do my eyes still ascend as long as

In deiner Schöne jugendlich blikst, und noch
    Zu herrlich nicht, zu stolz mir geworden bist,
        Du möchtest immer eilen, könnt ich,
            Göttlicher Wandrer, mit dir! Doch lächelst

Des frohen Ubermüthigen du, dass er
    Dir gleichen möchte; seegne mir lieber denn
        Mein sterblich Thun und heitre wieder,
            Gütiger! heute den stillen Pfad mir!

X. DA ICH EIN KNABE WAR

Da ich ein Knabe war,
Rettet' ein Gott mich oft
Vom Geschrei und der Ruthe der Menschen,
Da spielt' ich sicher und gut
Mit den Blumen des Hains,
Und die Lüftchen des Himmels
Spielten mit mir.

Und wie du das Herz
Der Pflanzen erfreust,
Wenn sie entgegen dir
Die zarten Arme streken,
So hast du mein Herz erfreut
Vater Helios! und, wie Endymion,
War ich dein Liebling,
Heilige Luna!

O all ihr treuen,
Freundlichen Götter!
Dass ihr wüsstet,
Wie euch meine Seele geliebt!

Zwar damals rieff ich noch nicht
Euch mit Nahmen, auch ihr
Nanntet mich nie, wie die Menschen sich nennen,
Als kennten sie sich.

You still seem young in all of your beauty, still
    Have grown not too resplendent and too superb;
        You might forever move if only,
            Celestial wanderer, I could join you!

You smile at such an exultant pride, that he
    Should long to resemble you; then rather bless
        My mortal deeds and once again, O
            Kindly one, brighten my quiet pathway.

X. YOUTH

Once when I was a boy
A saviour spared me
From the clamor and violence of men:
And safe and serene I
Played in the flowering grove,
The airs of the heavens
Played over me.

And, just as you gladden
The hearts of the flowers
As they sunward spread their
Delicate arms to you,
So you have gladdened my heart,
Father Helios! And like Endymion
I was your darling,
Heavenly Luna!

O all you faithful
And friendly deities!
If you could only
Know how my spirit adored you!

True, not yet did I call
You by name, nor did you give
Me a name, in the manner that men give
Names, as though they knew one another.

Doch kannt'ich euch besser
Als ich je die Menschen gekannt,
Ich verstand die Stille des Athers,
Der Menschen Worte verstand ich nie.

Mich erzog der Wohllaut
Des säuselnden Hains
Und lieben lernt' ich
Unter den Blumen.

Im Arme der Götter wuchs ich gross.

XI. HYPERIONS SCHIKSAALSLIED

Ihr wandelt droben im Licht
Auf weichem Boden, seelige Genien!
Glänzende Götterlüfte
Rühren euch leicht,
Wie die Finger der Künstlerin
Heilige Saiten.

Schiksaallos, wie der schlafende
Säugling, athmen die Himmlischen;
Keusch bewahrt
In bescheidener Knospe,
Blühet ewig
Ihnen der Geist,
Und die seeligen Augen
Bliken in stiller
Ewiger Klarheit.

Doch uns ist gegeben,
Auf keiner Stätte zu ruhn,
Es schwinden, es fallen
Die leidenden Menschen
Blindlings von einer
Stunde zur andern,
Wie Wasser von Klippe
Zu Klippe geworfen,
Jahr lang ins Ungewisse hinab.

Yet I knew you far better
Than I ever knew men;
Stillness of ether I understood,
But the words of men never.

I was raised by the gentle
Murmur of woods
And I learned to love
Among blossoms.

And I grew in the arms of the gods.

XI. HYPERION'S SONG

You wander high in the light
   Over the tender floor, O blessed spirits!
      Glistening airs of the gods
         Lightly caress you
            Like the musician's fingers
               On saintly strings.

Fateless, like the slumbering
   Babe, breathe the heavenly ones;
      Virginally preserved
         In its modest bud
            Their spirit
               Eternally blooms
                  And their blessèd eyes
                     Gaze in their long and
                        Lucid stillness.

Yet we are destined
   Never to come to rest;
      They falter, they fall,
         These suffering mortals,
            In blindness from
               One hour to the next
                  Like water hurled from
                     Cliff upon cliff
                        Down the whole year long into
                           the unfathomed.

XII. ABENDPHANTASIE

Vor seiner Hütte ruhig im Schatten sizt
    Der Pflüger; dem Genügsamen raucht sein Heerd.
        Gastfreundlich tönt dem Wanderer im
            Friedlichen Dorfe die Abendgloke.

Wohl kehren jezt die Schiffer zum Hafen auch,
    In fernen Städten fröhlich verrauscht des Markts
        Geschäfftger Lärm; in stiller Laube
            Glänzt das gesellige Mahl den Freunden.

Wohin denn ich? Es leben die Sterblichen
    Von Lohn und Arbeit; wechselnd in Müh und Ruh
        Ist alles freudig; warum schläft denn
            Nimmer nur mir in der Brust der Stachel?

Am Abendhimmel blühet ein Frühling auf;
    Unzählig blühn die Rosen, und ruhig scheint
        Die goldne Welt; o dorthin nehmt mich,
            Purpurne Wolken! und möge droben

In Licht und Luft zerrinnen mir Lieb und Laid!—
    Doch, wie verscheucht von thörichter Bitte, flieht
        Der Zauber; dunkel wirds, und einsam
            Unter dem Himmel, wie immer, bin ich.—

Komm du nun, sanfter Schlummer! zu viel begehrt
    Das Herz; doch endlich, Jugend, verglühst du ja,
        Du ruhelose, träumerische!
            Friedlich und heiter ist dann das Alter.

XII. EVENING FANTASY

Beneath the shaded calm of his cottage now
  The ploughman sits; the hearth of the frugal one
    Is smoking: peaceful tolls the village
      Bell for the traveller its evening welcome.

The ships return at last to their native ports
  And now subsides the noise of the marketplace
    In distant towns; in quiet arbors
      Supper gleams for the friendly gathering.

Where shall I go? On labor and wage must live
  All mortals; the alternation of work and rest
    Brings joy to all; ah why then does this
      Thorn in my heart never cease its aching?

A spring now flowers forth in the evening sky;
  The countless roses blossom and peaceful glows
    The golden world: O clouds of purple,
      Carry me with you! and in the ether

And light let grief and passion subside at last! . . .
  The magic, put to flight by the reckless plea,
    Departs; and darkness falls and lonely
      Under the heaven I stand as always.

Come now, sweet slumber, come! For the heart desires
  Too much; and yet your embers must fade at last,
    O youth, reposeless, visionary!
      Age then descends on us, calm, contented.

XIII. ANDENKEN

Der Nordost wehet,
Der liebste unter den Winden
Mir, weil er feurigen Geist
Und gute Fahrt verheisset den Schiffern.
Geh aber nun und grüsse
Die schöne Garonne,
Und die Gärten von Bourdeaux
Dort, wo am scharfen Ufer
Hingehet der Steg und in den Strom
Tief fällt der Bach, darüber aber
Hinschauet ein edel Paar
Von Eichen und Silberpappeln;

Noch denket das mir wohl und wie
Die breiten Gipfel neiget
Der Ulmwald, über die Mühl',
Im Hofe aber wächset ein Feigenbaum.
An Feiertagen gehn
Die braunen Frauen daselbst
Auf seidnen Boden,
Zur Märzenzeit,
Wenn gleich ist Nacht und Tag,
Und über langsamen Stegen,
Von goldenen Träumen schwer,
Einwiegende Lüfte ziehen.

Es reiche aber,
Des dunkeln Lichtes voll,
Mir einer den duftenden Becher,
Damit ich ruhen möge; denn süss
Wär' unter Schatten der Schlummer.
Nicht ist es gut
Seellos von sterblichen
Gedanken zu seyn. Doch gut
Ist ein Gespräch und zu sagen
Des Herzens Meinung, zu hören viel
Von Tagen der Lieb',
Und Thaten, welche geschehen.

XIII. REMINISCENCE

The northeast is blowing,
Dearest among the breezes
To me, since the lusty heart and the lucky
Voyage he promises to the sailors:
Go, go now and greet
The lovely Garonne
And the gardens of Bordeaux
Along whose sharp-edged shore
The path follows and deep
To the current falls the brook: and above
Gaze the noble twins,
The oak and the silver poplar;

There does my mind still dwell: how
The elm woods bow their broadening
Summits over the mill:
In the courtyard a figtree grows.
In holidays there wander
The women in brown
Over the silken floor,
And in March
When night and day grow equal
And over the gradual paths
Heavy with golden reveries
Caressive airs go roving.

O offer me
The fragrant goblet
Filled with the dusky light
That I may rest in peace; ah, sweet
To sleep among shadows!
To be soulless, filled with ephemeral
Thoughts is not good: good
Is the exchange of words, and to speak
Straight from the heart, and to hear
Of days spent in affection,
Of deeds truly fulfilled.

Wo aber sind die Freunde? Bellarmin
Mit dem Gefährten? Mancher
Trägt Scheue, an die Quelle zu gehn;
Es beginnet nemlich der Reichtum
Im Meere. Sie,
Wie Maler, bringen zusammern
Das Schöne der Erd' und verschmähn
Den geflügelten Krieg nicht, und
Zu wohnen einsam, jahrlang, unter
Dem entlaubten Mast, wo nicht die Nacht durchglänzen
Die Feiertage der Stadt,
Und Saitenspiel und eingeborener Tanz nicht.

Nun aber sind zu Indiern
Die Männer gegangen,
Dort an der luftigen Spiz'
An Traubenbergen, wo herab
Die Dordogne kommt
Und zusammen mit der prächt'gen
Garonne meerbreit
Ausgehet der Strom. Es nehmet aber
Und giebt Gedächtniss die See,
Und die Lieb' auch heftet fleissig die Augen.
Was bleibet aber, stiften die Dichter.

XIV. PATMOS
DEM LANDGRAFEN VON HOMBURG

Nah ist
Und schwer zu fassen der Gott.
Wo aber Gefahr ist, wächst
Das Rettende auch.
Im Finstern wohnen
Die Adler und furchtlos gehn
Die Söhne der Alpen über den Abgrund weg
Auf leichtgebaueten Brüken.

Ah, but where are the friends? Bellarmin
With his companion? Many a one
Feels shy on approaching the spring;
For indeed all wealth begins
In the seas. They
Like the painters, gather
The beauties of the earth and despise
Neither the wingèd war, nor
Dwelling alone, all year, under
The leafless mast, where never across the night
Glitter the festivals of the city
And the sound of strings, and the native dances.

Now for the Indies
All the men have departed,
And there to the breezy peak
Of the vine-laden hills, where downward
Runs the Dordogne
And together with the magnificent
Garonne, wide as the sea
The current emerges. But the sea
Our memories both withdraws and restores.
And love too seizes and holds our eyes.
Yet all that endures, is given to us by the poets.

XIV. PATMOS
TO THE LANDGRAVE OF HOMBURG

Near, near and
Difficult to grasp is the Almighty.
Yet where the danger lies, there
Likewise lies the salvation.
In darkness dwell
The eagles; fearless the sons
Of the Alps pass over the abyss
On delicate bridges.

Drum, da gehäuft sind rings
Die Gipfel der Zeit,
Und die Liebsten nahe wohnen, ermattend auf
Getrenntesten Bergen,
So gieb unschuldig Wasser,
O Fittige gieb uns, treuesten Sinns
Hinüberzugehn und wiederzukehren.

So sprach ich, da entführte
Mich schneller, denn ich vermuthet
Und weit, wohin ich nimmer
Zu kommen gedacht, ein Genius mich
Vom eigenen Hauss'. Es dämmerten
Im Zwielicht, da ich gieng,
Der schattige Wald
Und die sehnsüchtigen Bäche
Der Heimath; nimmer kannt' ich die Länder;
Doch bald, in frischem Glanze,
Geheimnissvoll
Im goldenen Rauche blühte
Schnellaufgewachsen
Mit Schritten der Sonne
Mit tausend Gipfeln duftend

Mir Asia auf, und geblendet sucht'
Ich eines, dass ich kennete, denn ungewohnt
War ich der breiten Gassen, wo herab
Vom Tmolus fährt
Der goldgeschmükte Pactol
Und Taurus stehet und Messogis,
Und voll von Blumen der Garten,
Ein stilles Feuer. Aber im Lichte
Blüht hoch der silberne Schnee;
Und Zeug' unsterblichen Lebens
An unzugangbaren Wänden
Uralt der Epheu wächst und getragen sind
Von lebenden Säulen, Cedern und Lorbeern
Die feierlichen,
Die göttlichgebauten Palläste.

Massed around us arise
The summits of time, and the dearest
Live close, yet exhausted
Among their separate hills:
Give to us guiltless water,
O give us wings, for the faithful
Voyage and the return!

Thus I spoke, and a spirit
Drew me away from my home
More swiftly than I had ever
Surmised, and far away, where I had never
Dreamed of arriving. Dim
Through the twilight shone as I passed
The shadowy wood
And the yearning streams
Of my home; and the land grew strange;
And soon, sparkling anew,
Mysterious among
The golden vapors, Asia
Arose, blossoming swiftly
Under the tread of the sun
And odorous with a thousand

Summits; and blinded I sought for
Something that I might know; for the broad
Lanes were unfamiliar, where down
From Tmolus the gilded
Paktol glides, and Taurus
Stands, and Messogis,
And the garden blazing with flowers
Like a soundless fire. But in the dawn
The towering snow blooms into silver;
And, witness to the immortal,
The ageless vines go winding
Over the inaccessible walls, and borne
By living pillars, cedar and laurel,
Rise the majestic
Palaces built by the gods.

Es rauschen aber um Asias Thore
Hinziehend da und dort
In ungewisser Meeresebene
Der schattenlosen Strassen genug,
Doch kennt die Inseln der Schiffer.
Und da ich hörte
Der nahegelegenen eine
Sei Patmos,
Verlangte mich sehr
Dort einzukehren und dort
Der dunkeln Grotte zu nahn.
Denn nicht, wie Cypros,
Die quellenreiche, oder
Der anderen eine
Wohnt herrlich Patmos

Gastfreundlich aber ist
Im ärmeren Hausse
Sie dennoch,
Und wenn vom Schiffbruch oder klagend
Um die Heimath oder
Den abgeschiedenen Freund
Ihr nahet einer
Der Fremden, hört sie es gern; und ihre Kinder,
Die Stimmen des heissen Hains,
Und wo der Sand fällt und sich spaltet
Des Feldes Fläche, die Laute
Sie hören ihn, und liebend tönt
Es wieder von den Klagen des Manns. So pflegte
Sie einst des gottgeliebten,
Des Sehers, der in seeliger Jugend war

Gegangen mit
Dem Sohne des Höchsten, unzertrennlich, denn
Es liebte der Gewittertragende die Einfalt
Des Jüngers und es sahe der achtsame Mann
Das Angesicht des Gottes genau,
Da, beim Geheimnisse des Weinstoks, sie
Zusammensassen, zu der Stunde des Gastmals

Many the shadowless streets
That rush past Asia's gates
And draw us headlong
Into the fathomless plains of the sea:
Yet the skipper knows the isles.
And when I heard
That among the neighboring ones
Lay Patmos,
I was seized with desire
To journey there, and there
To visit the dusky grotto.
For unlike Cyprus,
Laden with springs, unlike
Any of these
In splendor Patmos dwells.

Nevertheless in her humbler
Home she offers
A welcome to guests,
And when the shipwrecked stranger
Or the stranger yearning
For home or the parted friend
Approaches her,
She smiles; and her children,
The voice of the sultry wood,
And the falling sand, and the splitting
Stretch of the fields, these sounds
All hear him, and tenderly
Echo the man's lament. For once she fostered
Him whom the god adored,
The seer, who once in his happy

Youth inseparably had wandered
With the son of the Almighty; for
The Bearer of Thunder had loved
The youth's simplicity, and the listening
Mortal gazed on the god's own features
As, among the mysteries of the vine, they
Sat together at suppertime, and his spacious

Und in der grossen Seele, ruhigahnend den Tod
Aussprach der Herr, und die lezte Liebe, denn nie genug
Hatt' er von Güte zu sagen
Der Worte, damals, und zu erheitern, da
Ers sahe, das Zürnen der Welt.
Denn alles ist gut. Drauf starb er. Vieles wäre
Zu sagen davon. Und es sahn ihn, wie er siegend blikte
Den Freudigsten die Freunde noch zulezt.

(Fragment)

XV. HÄLFTE DES LEBENS

Mit gelben Birnen hänget
Und voll mit wilden Rosen
Das Land in den See,
Ihr holden Schwäne,
Und trunken von Küssen
Tunkt ihr das Haupt
Ins heilignüchterne Wasser.

Weh mir, wo nehm' ich, wenn
Es Winter ist, die Blumen, und wo
Den Sonnenschein
Und Schatten der Erde?
Die Mauern stehn
Sprachlos und kalt, im Winde
Klirren die Fahnen.

Soul filled with a calm foreboding
Of death, and a final passion, the Master spoke: never
Did he tire of speaking of virtue, nor
Of consoling, whenever
He saw it, the wrath of the world.
For all things are good. And he died. Much
Might be said thereof. And his friends beheld him
At the end, as he gazed in triumph, happiest of all. . . .
(Fragment)

XV. THE HALF OF LIFE

Laden with yellowing pears
And with wild roses filled
Lies the land in the sea:
Beautiful swans,
Drunk with your kisses you
Dip your heads in the
Saintly sobering water.

Alas, where can I find, when
Winter arrives, the flowers? Where
The light of the sun
And the shadows of the earth?
The walls arise
Speechless and cold: in the wind
Clatter the banners.

"SOME POEMS OF FRIEDRICH HÖLDERLIN" HAS BEEN SET
IN JANSON AND CASLON TYPES AND
PRINTED AT THE SAMUEL MARCUS PRESS
CAMBRIDGE, MASSACHUSETTS
ORIGINAL DESIGN BY MARGARET EVANS

THE POETS OF THE YEAR

Series IV

SELECTED POEMS of *Herman Melville;* THIRTY POEMS *by Thomas Merton;* SELECTED POEMS of *Rafael Alberti* translated by *Lloyd Mallan;* THE SOLDIER *by Conrad Aiken;* SELECTIONS FROM THE NOTE-BOOKS of *Gerard Manley Hopkins;* THE HITLERIAD *by A. M. Klein.* ($3, boxed set of 6.)

Series III

NEW POEMS *by Dylan Thomas;* A SATIRE AGAINST MANKIND AND OTHER POEMS *by Rochester;* A LITTLE ANTHOLOGY OF CANADIAN POETS; POEMS, NEW AND SELECTED *by Richard Eberhart;* POEMS of *Hoelderlin;* THE TRIAL OF LUCULLUS *by Bertolt Brecht;* THE GIANT WEAPON *by Yvor Winters;* THREE RUSSIAN POETS translated by *Vladimir Nabokov;* SACRED AND SECULAR ELEGIES *by George Barker;* AND YOU, THOREAU *by August Derleth;* THE ILLUMINATIONS of *Rimbaud;* THE VIOLENT *by Harry Brown.* ($5.50, boxed set of 12.)